Developed and produced by Ripley Publishing Ltd

This edition published and distributed by:

Mason Crest
450 Parkway Drive, Suite D, Broomall, PA 19008
www.masoncrest.com

Printed and bound in the United States of America

First printing
9 8 7 6 5 4 3 2 1

Ripley's Believe It or Not!
Body Tales
ISBN: 978-1-4222-2775-6 (hardback)
ISBN: 978-1-4222-9036-1 (e-book)
Ripley's Believe It or Not!—Complete 8 Title Series
ISBN: 978-1-4222-2979-8

Cataloging-in-Publication Data on file with the Library of Congress

PUBLISHER'S NOTE
While every effort has been made to verify the accuracy of the entries in this book, the
Publishers cannot be held responsible for any errors contained in the work. They would
be glad to receive any information from readers.

WARNING
Some of the stunts and activities in this book are undertaken by experts and should not
be attempted by anyone without adequate training and supervision.

Strikingly True

BODY TALES

www.MasonCrest.com

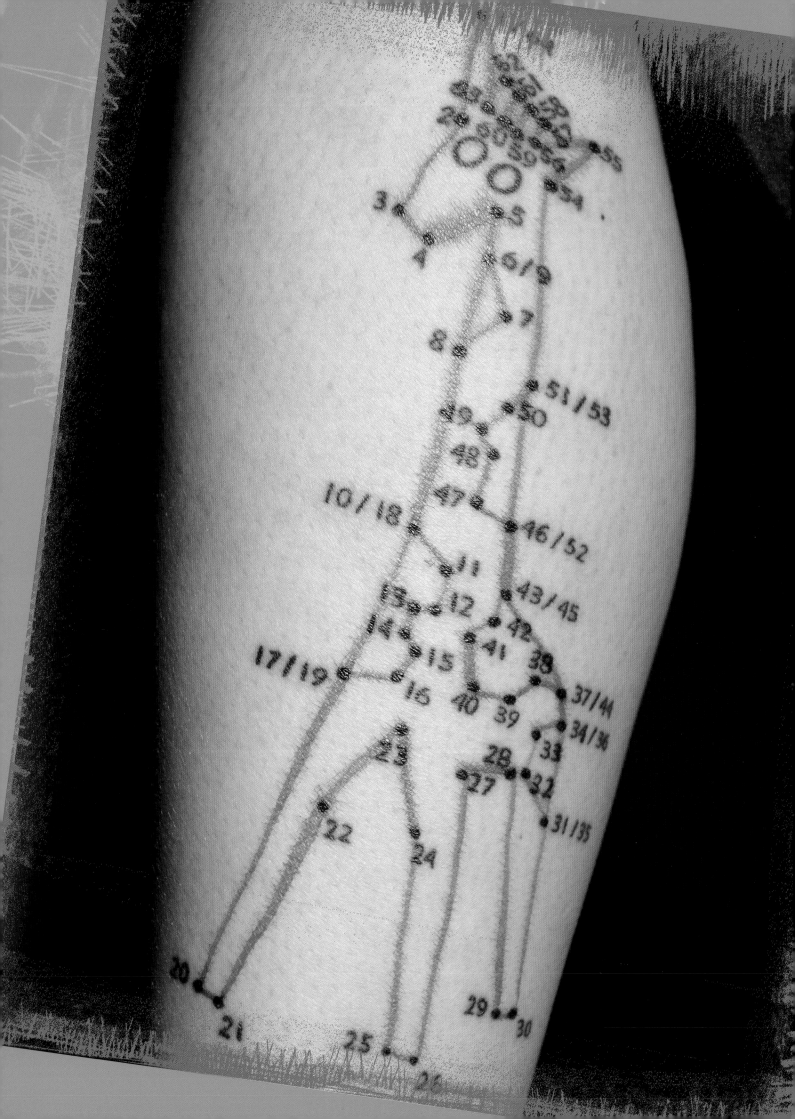

BODY TALES

Get a load of these amazing people! Read

about the amazing human body. Meet the

incredible 6-ft 9-in (2.06-m) teenager, the

woman with hair longer than a pickup truck,

and the boy who had eight toes on each foot.

*Colleen A. F. Venable has a
connect-the-dots tattoo shaped
like a giraffe on her leg...*

Major Mite

▼ At only 28 in (71 cm) tall when fully grown, Major Mite was no bigger than the average toddler.

▲ Major Mite would travel with his normal-sized parents Frank and Helen Howerton. Frank entered Major Mite in local sideshows before he was snapped up by the Ringling Brothers for their traveling circus. Each of his four brothers grew to be 6 ft (1.8 m) tall.

Clarence C. "Major Mite" Howerton was born in February 1913, and was billed by the press in the 1930s as the smallest man in the world. He stood only 28 in (71 cm) tall and weighed just 20 lb (9 kg). He was so small that he once traveled from New York to Chicago to find a tailor who would make a tuxedo for his diminutive size. He wore custom-made shoes just 2.5 in (6 cm) long.

The Ringling Brothers and Barnum & Bailey Circus signed up Major Mite in 1923, when he was ten years old, and he starred in its sideshow for more than 25 years. As well as being a big draw on the sideshow circuit, Major Mite featured in several Our Gang comedy shorts and played a trumpet-playing munchkin in the 1939 film The Wizard of Oz.

After a life in showbusiness, he died in Oregon at the age of 62.

MAJOR MITE
AGE 20 YEARS
WEIGHT 20 POUNDS
HEIGHT 26 INCHES

▲ The Ringling Brothers Circus was the biggest of its kind, featuring 800 performers and more than a thousand animals.

▼ Major Mite plays cards with 7-ft-8-in-tall (2.3-m) Jack Earle during downtime while performing for the Ringling Brothers Circus in the early 1930s.

▲ Tiny Major Mite being held aloft by his friend, giant Jack Earle.

• Clarence C. Howerton was not the only "Major Mite," although he was by far the most famous. A 33-in (84-cm) comedian who died in New York in 1900 also shared the name, as did other little people on the circus sideshow circuit.

• Major Mite became a mascot for the U.S. Marine Corps recruitment before retiring from the entertainment industry in 1948.

▲ Major Mite performed with many extreme individuals, such as 700-lb (318-kg) Ruth Pontico.

◀ Reports suggest that Major Mite had a rebellious streak, sometimes dressing in children's clothes and then shocking the public by smoking, shouting—or posing on a motorbike.

what knife? Julia Popova of Moscow, Russia, was attacked by a mugger in February 2010 but walked home not aware that she had been stabbed and that the knife was still impaled in her neck.

miss plastic A 2009 beauty contest in Budapest, Hungary, was open only to women who had undergone cosmetic surgery. "Miss Plastic" featured contestants who had enhanced their bodies with everything from new breasts and liposuction to hair transplants.

nasty shock In 2003, librarian Susanne Caro of Sante Fe, New Mexico, opened a 115-year-old medical book and found an envelope containing scabs from smallpox patients.

skeleton growth A person's skeleton continues to grow until around age 25, when the collarbone finally finishes developing.

strong boy Kyle Kane, a 12-year-old schoolboy from the West Midlands, England, lifted a 308-lb (140-kg) weight—more than twice his own body weight—at a junior bodybuilding event in 2010.

HUMAN SKELETON

Billed as the "Skeleton Dude" at Coney Island's Dreamland Circus in 1917, Eddie Masher of Brooklyn, New York, stood 5 ft 7 in (1.7 m) tall, but he declared he weighed just 38 lb (17 kg). Other records have put him at 48 lb (22 kg) or as much as 67 lb (30 kg), but even those weights were astonishingly light for an adult man. He was so skinny that tailors struggled to make a suit that would fit him. He died in 1962 at 70 years old—a good age for a skeleton!

secret bullet Vasily Simonov of Togliatti, Russia, has lived with a bullet in his lung for 70 years. As a child in 1941, he was playing with a rifle cartridge when he decided to take out the bullet and shove it up his nose. After trying in vain to remove it, he then breathed it in. He forgot all about it and the lodged bullet never caused him any problems, only coming to light during an MRI scan in 2009. Even then, doctors decided it was best to leave the bullet where it was.

body sale In 2010, anatomist Gunther von Hagens launched a mail-order service for his Plastinarium museum in the German town of Guben, selling human and animal body parts that had been preserved with a special plastic solution. Items for sale included a smoker's lung ($4,440), a chunk of human head ($2,000), a slice of a human hand ($228), and a cross-section of giraffe neck (price unspecified).

BIG BABY

At age two, Fan Sijia of Yuncheng City, Shanxi Province, China, was 3 ft 7 in (1.1 m) tall and weighed 100 lb (45 kg)—about four times the average weight for a girl her age.

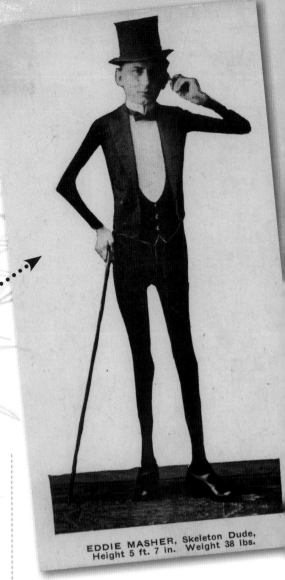

EDDIE MASHER, Skeleton Dude, Height 5 ft. 7 in. Weight 38 lbs.

kept "dying" Motorcyclist Steven Nixon from Derbyshire, England, suffered a massive heart attack after being in a collision with a car—but he pulled through even though he had technically "died" 28 times over the next few hours when his heart repeatedly stopped beating.

tall guy Sultan Kosen of Turkey stands 8 ft 1 in (2.5 m) tall. His hands measure 10¾ in (27.5 cm) and his feet 14⅓ in (36.5 cm). He lives with his parents, three brothers, and a sister, all of whom are of normal height and normal size.

bionic bottom After suffering massive internal injuries in a motorcycle crash, a man from South Yorkshire, England, now presses a remote control to open his bowels and go to the toilet. Surgeons rebuilt his bottom by taking a muscle from above his knee, wrapping it around his sphincter, and then attaching electrodes to the nerves. The electrodes are operated by a handset that he carries in his pocket and switches to on or off to control his bowel movements.

constantly seasick Jane Houghton from Cheshire, England, went on a week-long Mediterranean cruise—and still feels permanently seasick more than nine years later. She suffers from the rare Mal de Debarquement Syndrome, which causes people to feel as though they are constantly bobbing about on a rough sea. She feels so nauseous and wobbly that she has even had to stop buying clothes with stripes or busy patterns because she is unable to focus to iron them.

chute terror Skydiver Paul Lewis survived after falling 3,000 ft (900 m) onto the roof of a hangar at Tilstock Airfield, Shropshire, England, in August 2009. His main parachute failed to open at 3,000 ft (900 m) and although his reserve chute opened at 2,000 ft (600 m), a problem caused him to spiral out of control from 1,000 ft (300 m) with the canopy only partially opened. Luckily, the parachute became snagged on the hangar roof, preventing him from plunging to the ground and almost certain death.

busy brain The number of neurons in your brain—100 billion—is about the same as the number of stars in our galaxy.

Twisted Tiger

Double contortionists Hassani Mohammed (right) and Lazarus Mwangi of Cirque Mother Africa bend over backward to entertain the audience at a show in Hamilton, New Zealand.

matching horns A Chinese grandmother who grew a 2.4-in (6-cm) horn on the left side of her forehead in 2009 began to develop a similar growth on the right side of her forehead a year later. Zhang Ruifang from Linlou has cutaneous horns—growths made of keratin, the same substance that makes up fingernails. Most cutaneous horns are just a few millimeters long, but occasionally they can extend a number of inches from the skin.

weight loss In January 2010, former postman Paul Mason of Suffolk, England, weighed 980 lb (444.5 kg)—but then he instantly lost 294 lb (133.5 kg) after undergoing gastric bypass surgery. The operation involved having part of his stomach stapled off so that all the food he eats goes into a small pouch, vastly restricting the amount he can consume. At his heaviest he ate 20,000 calories a day—eight times the amount needed by an average man.

coal-powered bike Sylvester H. Roper of Roxbury, Massachusetts, built a steam-powered velocipede in the 1860s that drove like a motorcycle but was instead fueled by coal.

teenage toddler Although she is old enough to drive a car, Brooke Greenberg of Reisterstown, Maryland, weighs just 16 lb (7.2 kg), is 30 in (75 cm) tall, and rides around in a stroller pushed by her mother. The teenager has the body and behavior of a tiny toddler, thought to be the result of a mutation in the genes that control her aging and development, and which has apparently left her frozen in time.

tooth test Scientists can determine the ages of people born after 1943 to within 18 months by examining the amount of radioactive carbon in their teeth, caused by above-ground nuclear weapons testing in the 1950s and 1960s.

Ripley's Believe It or Not!®

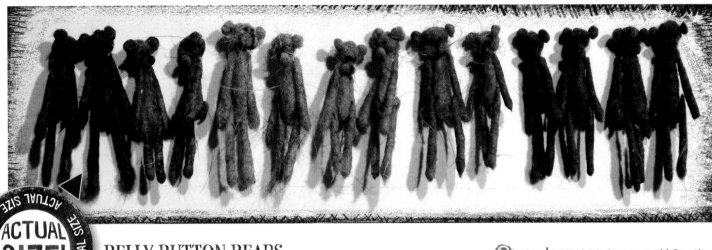

ACTUAL SIZE!

BELLY BUTTON BEARS

Artist Rachel Betty Case from Bethlehem, Pennsylvania, turns belly button fluff into tiny bears. She collects the lint from the belly buttons of male friends and sells her cute fluffy creations in small glass jars.

bullet surprise A 35-year-old Polish man who went to a hospital in Bochum, Germany, worried about a small lump on the back of his head, was unaware that he had been shot five years earlier. It was only when doctors removed a .22 caliber bullet that he remembered receiving a blow to the head around midnight at a New Year's Party.

metal muncher Doctors in Cajamarca, Peru, removed 2 lb 3 oz (1 kg) of metal from a man's stomach, including nails, coins, copper wire, and scrap metal. Requelme Abanto Alvarado said he had been eating metal for months and had once swallowed 17 5-in (13-cm) nails in one day.

talented toes Since having both arms amputated at age ten after an accident, Liu Wei of Beijing, China, has learned to do everything with his feet. He uses his toes to eat, dress himself, brush his teeth, and surf the Internet. He even plays the piano with his toes and earned a standing ovation when he performed on the TV show *China's Got Talent*, which he then went on to win.

not twins In 2010, Angie Cromar from Murray, Utah, found herself pregnant with two babies at the same time—but they weren't twins. She was born with a rare condition called didelphys, meaning two uteruses, and she conceived in both, at odds of one in five million.

long lobes Jian Tianjin, a farmer from Taiwan, has stretchy earlobes that make his ears 6½ in (16 cm) in length. His lobes are so long and flexible that they reach his shoulders and can be wound around his chin.

eight limbs Before having an operation to remove them when he was seven years old, Deepak Paswaan of Bihar, India, had four extra limbs—the result of being born with the arms, legs, and buttocks of a parasitic twin protruding from his chest. Although the parasitic twin's arms were small and withered, its legs grew at the same rate as Deepak, meaning the youngster had to carry a heavy weight around.

single handed Despite being born with just one hand, Kevin Shields from Fort William, Scotland, is an accomplished rock climber and has even mastered treacherous ice climbs.

GALL STONES

Doctors in Shenyang, Liaoning Province, China, removed more than 880 stones from the gall bladder of a 67-year-old woman. Mrs. Miao's gall bladder was so full of stones it had swollen to the size of a fist, forcing doctors to remove the whole bladder. They estimated that the stones had been forming inside her for about 20 years.

new language A 13-year-old Croatian girl woke from a 24-hour coma speaking fluent German. The girl was no longer able to speak Croatian but was able to communicate perfectly in German, a language that she had only just started studying at school.

sum girl! A 15-year-old schoolgirl with a love of math was awakened from a coma when her father began asking her simple sums. Vicki Alex of Northamptonshire, England, had been unconscious for three days and had failed to respond to other attempts to stimulate her brain, but after her father's intervention she soon regained full consciousness.

hairy hands Since becoming the first American to undergo a double hand transplant, Jeff Kepner from Augusta, Georgia, has noticed that his new hands are considerably hairier than the rest of his body because the donor had more hair than him.

self-amputation Ramlan, an 18-year-old construction worker who was trapped by a fallen concrete girder in the rubble of a building that collapsed during a 2009 earthquake in Padang, Indonesia, survived by sawing off his own leg.

toddler plunge Two-year-old Zhu Xinping had a miraculous escape after falling from the 21st floor of an apartment block in Jianyang City, Sichuan Province, China. She escaped with nothing worse than a broken leg after landing on a freshly dug pile of soil that cushioned her fall.

large family After giving birth to two sets of quadruplets (in 2004 and 2005), Dale Chalk of Sydney, New South Wales, Australia, had twins in 2009, giving her a total of 11 children under the age of seven.

self-service After badly cutting his leg in an accident at home, a 32-year-old man became so frustrated at having to wait an hour at Sundsvall Hospital in northern Sweden that he picked up a needle and thread and sewed up the cut himself.

tugged off In June 2009, a man from Shenzhen, China, was competing in a game of tug-of-war when he had his hand pulled off.

born twice Doctors in Texas performed prenatal surgery at 25 weeks to remove a grapefruit-sized tumor from Macie McCartney, while she was still inside her mother's womb. The procedure involved pulling out the uterus of mother Keri and then half of Macie's body out. Once free from the tumor, Macie was returned to the womb, where she recovered and grew for another ten weeks before being "born" again.

baby's tail Surgeons in China performed an operation to remove a 5-in-long (13-cm) tail from the body of a four-month-old baby girl. Hong Hong, from China's Anhui Province, was born with the tail, but it quickly doubled in size. X-rays had shown that it was connected to a fatty tumor within her spinal column.

reverse walker Rotating his feet nearly 180 degrees, Bittu Gandhi of Rajkot, Gujarat, India, can walk backward while facing forward!

Too Many Toes

In 2010, doctors at a hospital in Shenyang, China, operated on a six-year-old boy who had eight toes on each foot and 15 fingers owing to a rare genetic mutation known as central polydactyly. After a 6½-hour operation, medics had successfully removed 11 extra digits.

22cm

body tales
Believe It or Not!

determined dan Dan Netherland of Gatlinburg, Tennessee, can keep his fingers gripped together while ten people try to pull his arms apart.

tongue typist Legally blind and unable to use his hands, Josh LaRue of New Concord, Ohio, wrote a book by tapping out the words in Morse Code using his tongue.

lucky break When Raymond Curry overturned his car near his home in Northumberland, England, he was rushed to hospital with a fence post speared through his chest. There, doctors were relieved to see that the post had amazingly missed all of his vital organs—and they found a four-leafed clover stuck to his back.

saving lives Ben Kopp, a U.S. Army Ranger Corporal, was killed while saving six soldiers in a firefight and then helped save the lives of 75 others by donating his organs and tissues.

sprouting pea Doctors in Cape Cod, Massachusetts, investigating the cause of a patient's sickness, were stunned to find that he had a pea plant growing in his lung. They believe Ron Sveden, from nearby Brewster, had eaten a pea at some time in the previous couple of months but it had gone down the wrong way, and the seed had split inside him and started to sprout about ½ in (1 cm).

beatle tattoo Beatles fan Rose Ann Belluso of Downington, Pennsylvania, took a sign to Paul McCartney's Philadelphia show in August 2010 asking him to sign her back with a marker pen that she had brought along. After the singer called her up on stage and obliged, she decided to make the inscription permanent the next day by getting a tattoo artist to ink over the signature.

puff, puff... boom! Unlucky Andi Susanto of Indonesia lost six of his teeth when a cigarette he was smoking mysteriously exploded in February 2010.

route 66 Ron Jones of Bartlesville, Oklahoma, gets his kicks out of having Route 66 tattoos all over his body. He has more than 80 tattoos dedicated to destinations along the 2,448-mi (3,940-km) highway, including the Ariston Café in Litchfield, Illinois, and the arch on the Santa Monica Pier in California, which marks the end of the road.

bee therapy Bed-ridden multiple sclerosis sufferer Sami Chugg from Bristol, England, was able to get back on her feet after being stung 1,500 times by bees. The Bee Venom Therapy, carried out over a period of 18 months, involved holding a bee in a pair of tweezers and deliberately stinging an area of skin around her spine.

little miss dynamite Dr. Thienna Ho, 5 ft (1.5 m) tall and weighing barely 95 lb (43 kg), deadlifted 104,846 lb (47,557 kg) in one hour in San Francisco. The barbell she lifted weighed 46 lb (21 kg)—nearly half her body weight. She has previously completed more than 5,000 sumo squats in an hour.

chinese accent After suffering a severe migraine headache in March 2010, Sarah Colwill of Plymouth, Devon, England, suddenly started speaking with a Chinese accent—despite never having been to that country. Doctors say she has Foreign Accent Syndrome, a rare condition that damages the part of the brain that controls speech and word formation.

deep sleep A Polish man woke up from a 19-year coma to find the Communist Party no longer in power and food no longer rationed. After being hit by a train in 1988, railway worker Jan Grzebski also slept through the weddings of four of his children and the births of 11 grandchildren.

head returned Lewis Powell, a conspirator in the assassination of U.S. President Abraham Lincoln, was hanged in 1865 and was buried headless. His skull had been missing for 127 years when it was found in storage in the Smithsonian Museum and returned to the body.

migraine cure In order to relieve crippling migraine headache pains, teenager Melissa Peacock from Bradford, England, has to "drink" her brain fluid every day. At the age of nine she was diagnosed with intracranial hypertension, a condition that causes her body to produce too much spinal fluid. This collected in her skull and pushed on her brain, leaving her with such bad migraines and blurred vision that sometimes she could not walk in a straight line. On nine separate occasions, doctors punctured her skull to drain the fluid, but when it kept returning they decided to fit a tube that siphons fluid from her brain straight into her stomach.

odd reaction Desiree Jennings from Ashburn, Virginia, claimed she couldn't walk forward after suffering a freak reaction to a seasonal flu shot. Her forward motion suddenly became awkward with a twisted gait and she also had difficulty speaking, reading, and remembering things—yet the symptoms disappeared when she ran or walked backward.

frozen fingertip After losing her right pinky fingertip in an accident at her home in Davis, California, Deepa Kulkarni took it to doctors—and when they said they were unable to reattach it, she decided to investigate a new procedure called tissue regeneration. Eventually, she persuaded a local doctor to carry out tissue regeneration on her fingertip and after seven weeks of treatment it grew back. However, she still keeps the original fingertip in her freezer.

armless pitcher Tom Willis of San Diego, California, can throw a baseball the entire 60½ ft (18.5 m) distance from the mound to home plate without the ball bouncing—with his feet. Born with no arms, he has used his feet to throw the first pitch of a game at more than ten Major League Baseball stadiums in the United States.

hidden bullet Eighty-three-year-old World-War-II veteran Fred Gough from the West Midlands, England, thought that he was suffering from painful arthritis—until doctors told him in 2010 that a German bullet had been lodged in his hip for the past 66 years.

light lunch U.S. sideshow performer Todd Robbins has chewed and swallowed more than 4,000 lightbulbs.

bunny girl Rabbit-loving grandmother Annette Edwards of Worcester, England, has spent $16,000 on cosmetic surgery to make herself look like Jessica Rabbit, the sultry heroine of the 1988 movie *Who Framed Roger Rabbit?* As well as the surgery, she went on a rabbit-style diet for three months, eating just salads and cereals.

tattoo marathon In December 2009, Nick Thunberg was tattooed for 52 straight hours by body artist Jeremy Brown in Rockford, Illinois.

Self-styled

Etienne Dumont, a journalist from Geneva, Switzerland, has some of the most stunning body modifications in the world. He is tattooed from head to toe with vibrant images including skulls, flowers, and animals, but most striking are the designs covering his face and a hole stretched in his chin, held open by a transparent disk through which you can see his teeth. He also has a synthetic horn implant protruding from his scalp and has used progressively larger disks to stretch his earlobes.

body tales

Ripley's Believe It or Not!®

Iron Man

In 1848, a man working on the Vermont railway survived having an iron rod blasted right through his face and out of the top of his skull. Phineas Gage had been using explosives to clear space for the tracks by packing gunpowder into holes in rock with a heavy iron rod when a spark ignited the powder and the rod shot through his head.

Unbelievably, Gage survived this horrific accident and remained physically able for the rest of his life, although damage to his brain significantly altered his character. His injury became famous in medical circles, and contributed to an understanding of how the brain works. Gage returned to work as a coach driver and died in 1860, 12 years after his accident.

Identified as Gage in 2009, this photo shows him with the same 13-lb (6-kg) tamping iron that pierced his brain, which he kept as a gruesome souvenir. He lost the sight in his left eye when the rod passed behind it.

---

hair insured American football player Troy Polamalu, a defender with the Pittsburgh Steelers, has had his hair insured for $1 million by Lloyd's of London. His 3-ft-long (90-cm) black curls are so famous that he has not cut them since 2000. Although he wears a helmet while playing, his hair is still at risk—in 2006 he was tackled by his ponytail by Larry Johnson of the Kansas City Chiefs after intercepting a pass.

magnetic disruption Placing a magnet on your head can temporarily turn a right-handed person into a left-hander. By positioning a powerful magnet on the left posterior parietal cortex—a region of the brain that deals with planning and working out the relationship between three-dimensional objects—researchers at the University of California, Berkeley, found that normally right-handed volunteers started to use their left hand more frequently for tasks such as picking up a pencil. This is because the magnet disrupted and confused the volunteers' brains.

epic climb Three U.S. war veterans climbed 19,341-ft (5,895-m) Mount Kilimanjaro in Tanzania in 2010—despite having only one good leg between them. Amputees Dan Nevins, 37, of Jacksonville, Florida, who lost his legs in Iraq; Neil Duncan, 26, of Denver, Colorado, who lost both legs in a roadside bomb attack in Afghanistan; and Kirk Bauer, 62, of Ellicott City, Maryland, who lost a leg in Vietnam in 1969, made the climb on their prosthetic legs in just six days.

FACE BOOKED

In 2010, Chang Du from Lishuguo, China, went public with an offer to sell advertising space on his oversized chin. After a small pimple in his mouth swelled massively over a period of five years, Chang made the bizarre proposal in order to raise funds to reduce his chin back to normal size. He confirmed that an $8,000 offer would be enough to secure the space on his face.

fridge raider Anna Ryan of Blue Springs, Missouri, put on 126 lb (57 kg) over several years—by eating food from her refrigerator while sleepwalking. She was puzzled why her weight ballooned to 266 lb (121 kg) despite adhering to a strict low-fat diet. However, when she awoke one morning to find cookies in her bed it emerged that, unbeknown to her, she had been getting up regularly in the night to eat cheese, chocolate, and even meat.

human heads When airport workers in Little Rock, Arkansas, noticed a package that was not labeled properly, they checked the contents and found a shipment of 60 human heads. Further investigation revealed the heads were on their way to a company in Fort Worth, Texas, to be used by neurosurgeons for the study of ear, nose, and throat procedures.

heroic landing In early 2010, Lt. Ian Fortune of Britain's Royal Air Force was shot between the eyes while piloting a helicopter in Afghanistan. He survived the incident and continued flying for another eight minutes before making a successful landing, saving all 20 people on board.

full bladder After a 14-year-old boy in India was admitted to hospital complaining of pain and urinary problems, doctors were shocked to find a ¾-in-long (2-cm) fish in his bladder.

sucked hair After her car swerved off the road in Colorado, Cynthia Hoover survived for five days in the freezing wilderness of the Rocky Mountains by sucking water from her wet hair into her mouth. She was eventually found because she managed to crawl 450 yd (410 m)—despite having 11 broken ribs, a punctured lung, and several broken vertebrae—to where she heard voices coming from a disused mine.

snowshoe beard David Traver of Anchorage, Alaska, was the winner of the 2009 World Beard and Moustache Championships with his 20½-in-long (52-cm) beard woven to resemble a snowshoe.

Ripley's Ask

what is the best thing about having such long hair?
My long locks are my pride and joy and my baby. They can be bundled and used as an extra pillow. I also bundle them behind my lower back when driving long distance, because they work better than a pillow for back support. They work as a great scarf in the winter when I visit cold states.

How do you keep your hair under control on a day-to-day basis?
For chores and running errands, I tie my locks in a wrap on my lower back, just like African women carry their babies. It secures my locks and allows me total freedom of movement, which is brilliant as I am very over-protective of my locks.

How often do you wash it, and how long does that take? For 20 years I washed my locks three times a week. Now I wash them only once a week, as per advice from a locks stylist. It takes about 30 minutes to wash them, about 40 minutes wrapped in a huge bath towel to absorb the water, and between 15 and 24 hours to totally dry.

Would you ever get your hair cut? Never is a strong word, but I will NEVER cut my locks. My locks are my baby...my crown...they hold 22 years of my sorrows and my joys, they're like another person...yet it's me...no, I will never cut my locks.

celebrity tattoos Steve Porter from Nottingham, England, has 12 autographed pictures of celebrities—including Alice Cooper, Anastacia, and Ozzy Osbourne—inked onto his skin as tattoos. In total, he has more than 20 tattoos of actors and rock stars covering his body.

body bacteria There are as many as ten times the number of living bacteria and bugs in and on our bodies as there are human cells. Of the estimated 100 trillion microbes, the most densely populated areas of flesh are the belly button, the bottoms of the feet, and between the fingers.

still singing After suffering a stroke, singer Ann Arscott of Birmingham, England, was left unable to speak—but she could still sing. She has aphasia, a condition caused by damage to the areas of the brain responsible for language. It impairs speech, but some people with it can still sing, as music activates a different part of the brain.

cat boy A boy in Dahua, China, has bright blue eyes that glow in the dark and enable him to see in the pitch black. Nong Youhui can read perfectly in complete darkness and also has good vision during the day. Medical experts think he was born with a rare condition called leukodermia, which has left his eyes with less protective pigment and made them more sensitive to light.

sneezed nail Prax Sanchez, 72, of Colorado Springs, Colorado, had an MRI scan for an ear problem, which dislodged a nail in his head that he then coughed up after the procedure. He had no idea the nail was there and it could have been decades old.

LONG LOCKS
Asha Mandela from Clermont, Florida, has hair that measures an incredible 19 ft 6 in (6 m), longer than a pickup truck. Asha has not cut her hair for an astonishing 22 years.

Beautiful Bite

To enhance their beauty, women in the Mentawai Islands of Indonesia have their teeth filed into sharp points. The unusual rite of passage, in which the teeth are chiseled into shape with no anesthetic, conforms to local opinions of beauty rather than any practical purpose. Observers have commented that Mentawai women seem to feel no pain during the process, and that they willingly undergo the ritual.

back to life A 73-year-old woman was brought back to life 30 minutes after her heart stopped beating during a hospital test in Changsha, China. Usually a person dies if they cannot be revived within six minutes.

seven-foot worm Sailing on board the ship *Elizabeth* from Cork, Ireland, to Quebec, Canada, in June 1825, 12-year-old Ellen McCarthy fell ill and coughed up three intestinal worms, the longest of which measured 7 ft 3 in (2.2 m).

Ice Man Wearing just trunks, goggles, and a swimming cap, Lewis Pugh of Devon, England, swam 0.62 mi (1 km) across the glacial Pumori Lake, which lies 17,400 ft (5,300 m) up Mount Everest and has a water temperature of just 35°F (2°C). The man, dubbed the "human polar bear," took 22 minutes 51 seconds to breaststroke across the lake. He had to find a delicate balance between going too fast and going too slowly—too quickly he could have lost energy and drowned, but too slowly and he would have suffered hypothermia.

lightning strike Dog-walker Brad Gifford of Kettering, England, had a miraculous escape after he was knocked unconscious, burst both eardrums, and exploded into flames when a 300,000-volt bolt of lightning struck him on the ear. The lightning was traveling at 14,000 mph (22,500 km/h) and had heated the air around it to 54,032°F (30,000°C)—five times hotter than the surface of the Sun.

big baby At ten months old, Lei Lei, a baby from Hunan Province, China, weighed 44 lb (20 kg)—equivalent to the weight of an average six-year-old.

parachute plunge When her parachute became entangled seconds after she exited an airplane above South Africa, skydiver Lareece Butler plunged 3,000 ft (915 m) before hitting the ground—she survived with a broken leg, broken pelvis, bruises, and concussion.

ate finger In a protest over unpaid wages, a Serbian union official chopped off his finger and ate it. Zoran Bulatovic, a union leader at a textile factory in Novi Pazar, was so angry because some of his fellow workers had not been paid for several years that he used a hacksaw to chop off most of the little finger on his left hand and then ate it to underline the fact that the workers could no longer afford to eat conventional food.

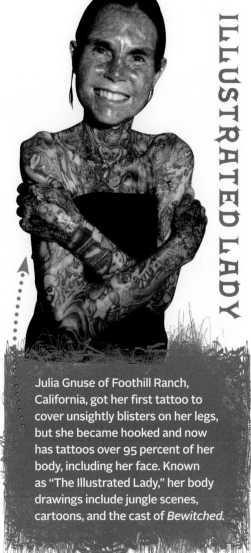

Julia Gnuse of Foothill Ranch, California, got her first tattoo to cover unsightly blisters on her legs, but she became hooked and now has tattoos over 95 percent of her body, including her face. Known as "The Illustrated Lady," her body drawings include jungle scenes, cartoons, and the cast of *Bewitched*.

MAGNETIC FINGERS

By having tiny magnetic implants inserted in their fingers, people are able to pick up metal items, such as paper clips or bottle tops, seemingly by magic. Some people have even had magnets inserted in the backs of their hands or on their ears!

RIPLEY RESEARCH

A small incision is made either at the front or to the side of the fingertip, a tiny dermal elevator is used to separate the layers of the skin, and then the magnet covered in silicone is inserted slightly to the side of the finger pad. The incision is then closed with a stitch. With a finger magnet, people can detect live electrical cables but they can't erase computer hard drives or credit cards or get stuck to refrigerators. The magnets are effective at lifting small items, but this shouldn't be done for longer than 20 minutes at a time in case the skin over the magnet becomes damaged.

HEADS OF STATE

Chinese micro-artist Jin Y. Hua has painted the face of every President of the United States from George Washington to George W. Bush—that's 42 portraits—on a single human hair less than ½ in (1.3 cm) long and just 0.0035 in (0.09 mm) thick. Jin uses a brush made from a single rabbit hair to apply the paint.

Thomas Jefferson 1801–1809

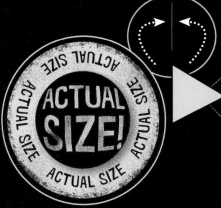

ACTUAL SIZE!

Lyndon B. Johnson 1963–1969

Ronald Reagan 1981–1989

George Washington 1789–1797

John Adams 1797–1801

Thomas Jefferson 1801–1809

James Madison 1809–1817

James Monroe 1817–1825

John Quincy Adams 1825–1829

Andrew Jackson 1829–1837

Martin Van Buren 1837–1841

William Henry Harrison 1841

John Tyler 1841–1845

James K. Polk 1845–1849

Zachary Taylor 1849–1850

Millard Fillmore 1850–1853

Franklin Pierce 1853–1857

James Buchanan 1857–1861

Abraham Lincoln 1861–1865

Andrew Johnson 1865–1869

Ulysses S. Grant 1869–1877

Rutherford B. Hayes 1877–1881

James A. Garfield 1881

Chester A. Arthur 1881–1885

Grover Cleveland 1885–1889 & 1893–1897

Benjamin Harrison 1889–1893

William McKinley 1897–1901

Theodore Roosevelt 1901–1909

William Howard Taft 1909–1913

Woodrow Wilson 1913–1921

Warren G. Harding 1921–1923

Calvin Coolidge 1923–1929

Herbert Hoover 1929–1933

Franklin D. Roosevelt 1933–1945

Harry S. Truman 1945–1953

Dwight D. Eisenhower 1953–1961

John F. Kennedy 1961–1963

Lyndon B. Johnson 1963–1969

Richard Nixon 1969–1974

Gerald Ford 1974–1977

Jimmy Carter 1977–1981

Ronald Reagan 1981–1989

George H. W. Bush 1989–1993

Bill Clinton 1993–2001

George W. Bush 2001–2009

John F. Kennedy 1961–1963

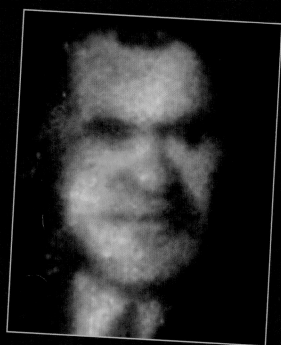

Richard Nixon 1969–1974

snake twins In June 2009, in Xiaogan, eastern China, Hui Chung gave birth to conjoined twins, who were known as the "snake babies" because they were attached at the waist. The siblings shared one long body with a head at each end, and as they did not have external sexual organs, it was impossible to say what sex they were.

long hair When 79-year-old Tran Van Hay died in Kien Giang, Vietnam, in February 2010, his hair was more than 22 ft (6.7 m) long and weighed 23 lb (10.5 kg). He began to let his hair grow more than 50 years ago, because he often became sick after a haircut. As his hair grew, he balanced it on his head like a basket.

LICK OFF

Actor Nick Afanasiev from California has an incredible role all to himself—as the owner of America's longest tongue! Stretching to an unbelievable 3.5 in (9 cm), it means that Nick can lick his own nose and even his elbow, a bizarre feat that most people find impossible.

BLOOD, SWEAT, AND TEARS

Twinkle Dwivedi from Lucknow, India, is one of the strangest and rarest medical cases in the world. From the age of 12, Twinkle began to bleed at random through the skin on any part of her body—without any visible wounds or pain—from the soles of her feet to her eyes. Although the cause of her spontaneous bleeding remains a mystery, experts believe that she may suffer from the blood disorder hematohidrosis, an extremely rare but recognized condition where the patient sweats blood through the skin.

miracle escape A Japanese toddler who wandered onto rail tracks in Suzaka City escaped with only scratches after a train came to a halt on top of her. After spotting the girl, the driver applied the emergency brakes and the train stopped with the girl beneath. She survived because she was trapped in the 20-in (50-cm) gap between the train and the tracks.

scorched footprints For two weeks in 2009, Sikeli Nadiri left a trail of scorched footprints on grassland around his home village in Fiji. There was no explanation as to why the grass had burned away beneath his feet, as he had not stepped on any chemicals or anything else that would cause scorching.

dangerous operation In March 2010, U.S. Army medical staff at Bagram airfield in Afghanistan donned armor in the operating room while removing a live high-explosive round from the scalp of a soldier from the Afghan Army.

Ripley's
Believe It or Not!®
baby tales

baby frozen Sixteen-week-old Finley Burton of County Durham, England, was put in a hospital "deep freeze" for four days to keep him alive when complications arose after heart surgery. His heart had started to beat alarmingly quickly, so his body was placed in a "cool bag," through which cold air was pumped to keep his temperature down. This slowed his metabolism, which in turn slowed his heart rate.

rare quads In December 2009, Lisa Kelly of Middlesbrough, England, gave birth to a set of quadruplets made up of two sets of identical twins—a ten-million-to-one chance!

vulture tonic In southern Africa, vultures' brains have become so popular as a traditional medicine that it has contributed to seven of the region's nine vulture species becoming endangered.

DENTAL DIRT
This is what your used dental floss looks like when magnified more than 500 times. Dental plaque, formed from bacteria and saliva, is clearly visible on the tiny floss fibers. Photographer Steve Gschmeissner from Bedford, England, used an electron microscope capable of magnifying objects more than 500,000 times to show everyday household items in a completely new light.

tiny tot A premature baby boy born at the University of Goettingen Hospital, Germany, in 2009 survived despite weighing less than 10 oz (283 g) at birth. The tiny tot weighed just 9.7 oz (275 g)—which is 75 grams below the weight doctors consider the minimum birth weight for a baby to survive.

kangaroo care Having been told by doctors at a hospital in Sydney, Australia, that her premature baby Jamie had not survived the birth, Kate Ogg cuddled her lifeless son—born at 27 weeks and weighing just 2 lb (900 g)—next to her body and said her tearful goodbyes to him. Incredibly, after two hours of being hugged, touched, and spoken to by his mother, baby Jamie began showing signs of life and was soon breathing normally and opening his eyes. The doctors called it a miracle but Kate put it down to "kangaroo care," a technique named after the way kangaroos hold their young in a pouch next to their body, allowing the mother to act as a living incubator and keep the baby warm.

knife horror Xiao Wei, a 16-year-old from Jilin, China, had a knife stabbed through his head that went in one side and out the other—but he survived after a two-hour operation to remove the blade.

canadian citizen On December 31, 2008, a Ugandan woman gave birth on an airplane flying over Nova Scotia, Canada. Her newborn daughter was granted Canadian citizenship.

scaly growths Muhammad Yunusov from Kyrgyzstan was born with the rare skin condition *Granulomatous candidiasis*, which left his face and head covered in scaly barnacle-like growths. Cruelly dubbed "dragon boy," he never went out without wearing a mask to cover his face. After six years of torment, he was finally cured when a dermatologist got rid of the unsightly growths in just 17 days with a mixture of creams and medication.

parasitic twin Eighteen-month-old Kang Mengru of Henan Province, China, had her dead twin removed from her stomach. Her parents were puzzled by her increasingly swollen stomach, which made her look pregnant, until medical scans revealed that she was carrying the parasitic fetus of her unborn twin in her belly. In such rare cases—affecting one in 500,000 births—one twin in the womb grows larger than the other and envelops its smaller sibling. The second fetus never fully develops, but continues to grow within the first baby, feeding off it like a parasite.

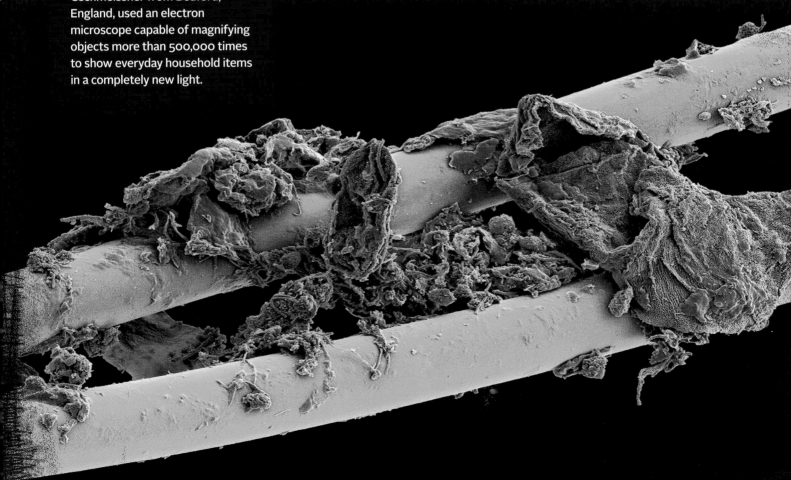

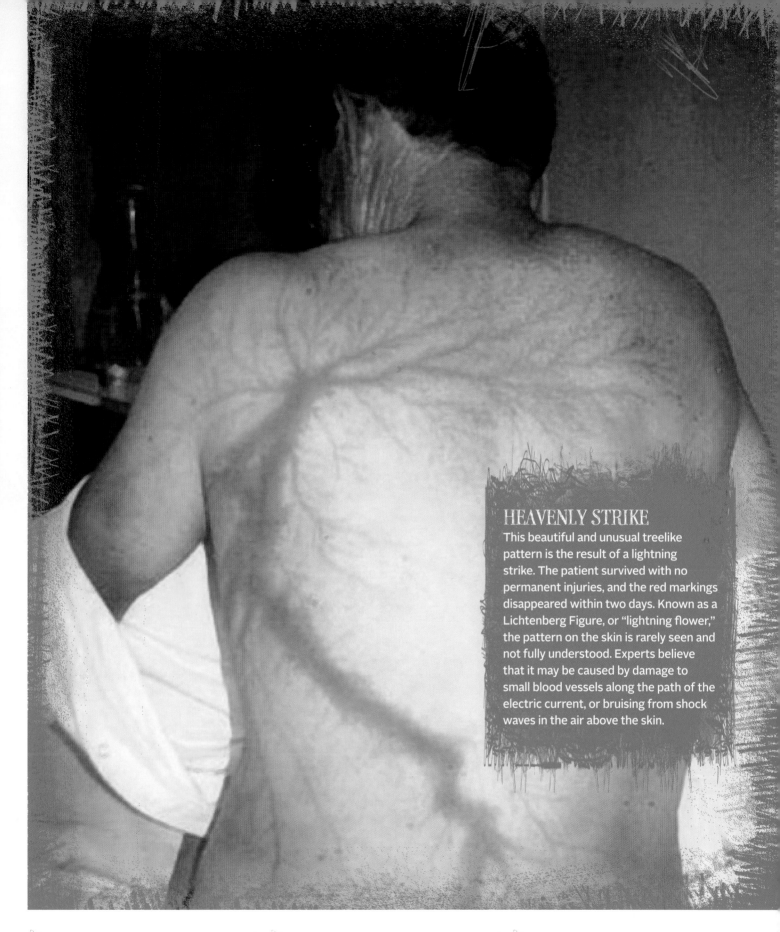

HEAVENLY STRIKE

This beautiful and unusual treelike pattern is the result of a lightning strike. The patient survived with no permanent injuries, and the red markings disappeared within two days. Known as a Lichtenberg Figure, or "lightning flower," the pattern on the skin is rarely seen and not fully understood. Experts believe that it may be caused by damage to small blood vessels along the path of the electric current, or bruising from shock waves in the air above the skin.

star wars tattoos *Star Wars* fan Luke Kaye from Wiltshire, England, has undergone more than 100 hours of pain to have his body tattooed. His back, arms, and legs are covered with tattoos of over a dozen characters from all six *Star Wars* movies, including Luke Skywalker, C-3PO, and Darth Vader.

churchill's chompers A pair of gold-plated false teeth owned by former British Prime Minister Winston Churchill sold at auction for £15,000 in 2010. Without his dentures, Churchill would never have been able to make his rousing wartime speeches—in fact, they were so valuable to him that he carried a spare set at all times.

human magnet Metal items such as coins, keys, safety pins, and spanners can stick to the body of 50-year-old Brenda Allison from London, England, for up to 45 minutes without falling off. All through her life, her mysterious magnetic powers have set off car alarms, interrupted TV signals, and blown out lightbulbs.

A Bicycle Made

...for Two

Although Charles B. Tripp had no arms and Eli Bowen had no legs, they were able to ride a bicycle—together. Known to circus audiences as "The Armless Wonder" and "The Legless Wonder," they simply combined their physical attributes on a tandem bicycle—Tripp pedaling with his legs and Bowen steering with his arms.

Charles B. Tripp was born without arms in 1855 in Woodstock, Ontario, Canada, but soon learned to dress himself and write using his feet. Remarkably, he made his living as a skilled carpenter until joining Barnum's Circus, which was the start of a 50-year career as a performer. He specialized in penmanship, portrait painting, and paper cutting—holding the implements between his toes. Around the turn of the century, he developed an interest in photography and became known as "The Armless Photographer." He died in 1939 in Salisbury, North Carolina, at the grand age of 84.

Eli Bowen was born in Ohio in 1844. He was one of ten children, all of whom were able-bodied except for Eli who had seal limbs, or phocomelia, a condition that left him with no legs and with two feet of different sizes growing from his hips. As a child he walked on his arms, perfecting a technique whereby he held wooden blocks in his hands that enabled him to swing his hips between his arms. The strength he gained from this helped him become a talented acrobat and, at the age of 13, he joined his first circus troupe. Despite his condition, Eli was considered by many to be the most handsome man in showbusiness and, at age 26, he married Mattie Haight who was ten years his junior. The couple had four healthy sons. He continued performing into his eighties, and his death, from pleurisy in 1924, was just days before he was due to appear at The Dreamland Circus at Coney Island, New York.

Eli Bowen with his wife and son

Charles Tripp having a cup of tea

body tales
Ripley's Believe It or Not!®

RUSTY NAIL

A man had a rusty 4.7-in-long (12-cm) nail removed from his left kidney in Zhengzhou, Henan Province, China. The nail had been in Mr. Gao's body for 20 years following an accident at home. Although it had cut into his stomach and entered his body, he had sterilized the wound and it healed. In time, a membrane formed around the nail, preventing it penetrating deeper into his body.

glass eater Wang Xianjun of Sichuan Province, China, has eaten more than 1,500 lightbulbs. He started snacking on broken glass when he was 12 because it was "crispy and delicious," and now regularly eats a bulb for breakfast. He smashes the bulb and swallows it piece by piece while sipping from a glass of water. Although his bizarre diet has apparently not affected his health, it did cost him his marriage. He had kept his glass munching a secret from his wife, but when she caught him, she thought it was too weird and they separated.

blood camp The Indian political party Shiv Sena collected 24,200 bottles of blood in a single day at a blood donation camp in Goregaon.

impaled by tree A 13-in-long (33-cm) tree limb crashed through the windshield as Michelle Childers of Kamiah, Idaho, and her husband were driving down the road, impaling her through the neck. Amazingly, she survived.

titanic tumor Doctors in Buenos Aires, Argentina, removed an enormous tumor weighing 50 lb 11 oz (23 kg) from the womb of a 54-year-old woman in 2010. It had been growing inside her body for 18 months. She entered a hospital for the operation weighing 308 lb (140 kg), but after the removal of the tumor she was discharged weighing just 231 lb (105 kg).

saved by implants When a gunman opened fire with a semiautomatic assault rifle in a dentist's office in Beverly Hills, California, Lydia Carranza's life was saved by her size-D breast implants, which took the force of the blow and stopped bullet fragments from reaching her vital organs.

sticky situation Irmgard Holm, 70, of Phoenix, Arizona, sealed her eye shut after mistakenly using quick-drying glue instead of eye drops. She had confused the two products' similar-looking bottles. Doctors cut off the glue covering her eye and washed out the remainder to prevent serious damage.

MONSTER STONE

A kidney stone the size of a coconut was removed by surgeons in Hungary from the stomach of Sandor Sarkadi. Whereas even the largest kidney stones are seldom bigger than a golf ball, this one measured a whopping 6¾ in (17 cm) in diameter and weighed 2½ lb (1.1 kg).

Kidney Hoard

In an operation that took four hours, doctors in Dhule, India, removed a staggering 172,155 kidney stones from the left kidney of 45-year-old Dhranraj Wadile in December 2009.

guardian angel Angel Alvarez survived despite being shot 23 times by New York City police officers during a disturbance in August 2010. Although he was shot in the arms, legs, abdomen, and jaw, all the bullets somehow missed his vital organs.

self-amputation Jonathan Metz of West Hartford, Connecticut, saved his own life by partially sawing off his left arm after it had become trapped in his furnace boiler and started to turn gangrenous. Taking a blade from his toolbox, he began sawing through the arm to prevent the infection spreading to the rest of his body. To stem the flow of blood, he used first his shirt and then a telephone cord as a tourniquet. After more than two days—during which his only drink was rust-colored boiler water scooped into his mouth with a flip-flop he had been wearing—he was rescued and taken to hospital where doctors completed the amputation.

reading mystery On July 31, 2001, Canadian mystery writer Howard Engel awoke from a stroke and discovered he could no longer read—but could still write. He was diagnosed as having *alexia sine agraphia*, which meant that newspapers and even his own books appeared to be written in indecipherable oriental script.

supersized son At age three, Xiao Hao of Guangzhou, China, weighs a massive 140 lb (63.5 kg)—as much as an adult man. He dwarfs his mom and has been banned by some nurseries as a hazard to other children.

lucky bounce An 18-month-old boy escaped without a scratch after falling 80 ft (24.4m) from his seventh-floor apartment in Paris, France, bouncing off a café awning and into the arms of a passing doctor. The café was closed for the day and the awning was out only because a mechanism had jammed.

deadly device U.S. Army Private Channing Moss survived a direct body hit from an anti-vehicular rocket in Afghanistan. Luckily, the explosive head failed to detonate, but he was impaled by the rocket shaft.

on the run Former British Army soldier Mike Buss from Swindon, England, completed 517¼ mi (832.4 km) on a treadmill over seven grueling days. He ran the equivalent of nearly three marathons a day, sleeping for just two hours a day, and lost two toenails in the process.

Foreign Bodies

- SURGEONS IN CHINA FOUND A PIECE OF GRASS, 1³/₁₆ IN (3 CM) LONG, GROWING IN THE LUNG OF A TEN-MONTH-OLD BABY GIRL.

- AFTER SWALLOWING A BONE AT DINNER, A CALIFORNIAN BOY HAD IT STUCK IN HIS LUNG FOR THE NEXT 11 YEARS.

- A FRAGMENT OF A PLASTIC EATING UTENSIL WAS FOUND IN THE LEFT LUNG OF JOHN MANLEY FROM WILMINGTON, NORTH CAROLINA. HE HAD INHALED IT TWO YEARS EARLIER WHILE EATING AT A FAST-FOOD RESTAURANT.

- QIN YUAN FROM CHONGQING, CHINA, ACCIDENTALLY SWALLOWED HIS FALSE TEETH, WHICH WERE LATER FOUND LODGED IN ONE OF HIS LUNGS.

- SURGEONS IN INDIA REMOVED A TOOTHBRUSH FROM THE STOMACH OF ANIL KUMAR, WHO HAD ACCIDENTALLY SWALLOWED IT WHILE BRUSHING HIS TEETH IN FRONT OF THE TV.

- DEREK KIRCHEN FROM NORFOLK, ENGLAND, HAD A CASHEW NUT STUCK IN HIS LUNG FOR 18 MONTHS.

- A SMALL BRANCH OF WHITE CEDAR WAS FOUND IN THE LUNG OF A 61-YEAR-OLD JAPANESE WOMAN.

- CHRIS BROWN OF GLOUCESTERSHIRE, ENGLAND, COUGHED UP A 1-IN-LONG (2.5-CM) TWIG THAT HAD BEEN WEDGED IN HIS LUNG FOR 20 YEARS.

- A 62-YEAR-OLD FRENCHMAN SWALLOWED 350 COINS, AN ASSORTMENT OF NECKLACES, AND SEVERAL NEEDLES. THE INGESTED MASS WEIGHED 12 LB 2 OZ (5.5 KG)—THE EQUIVALENT OF A BOWLING BALL—AND WAS SO HEAVY THAT IT HAD PUSHED THE MAN'S STOMACH BETWEEN HIS HIPS.

WEIRD INHALATION

After Artyom Sidorkin started coughing blood and complaining of chest pains, surgeons in Russia found a 2-in-long (5-cm) spruce tree inside his lung. He must have inhaled the piece of tree, which then got lodged in his lung, causing it to become seriously inflamed.

Accidental Discovery

X-rays were first observed in 1895 by German physicist Wilhelm Roentgen, who found them accidentally while experimenting with vacuum tubes. A form of electromagnetic radiation, they have gone on to become one of the most useful tools in medical history, employed for identifying everything from broken bones to accidentally swallowed toothbrushes.

chopstick removal A Chinese man had a chopstick removed from his stomach 28 years after swallowing it. Mr. Zhang had swallowed the chopstick in 1982, but thought it had been digested until he started suffering stomach pains. X-rays revealed that the remains of the chopstick were still inside him. Surgeons in Shanghai extricated it by making a small incision in his stomach.

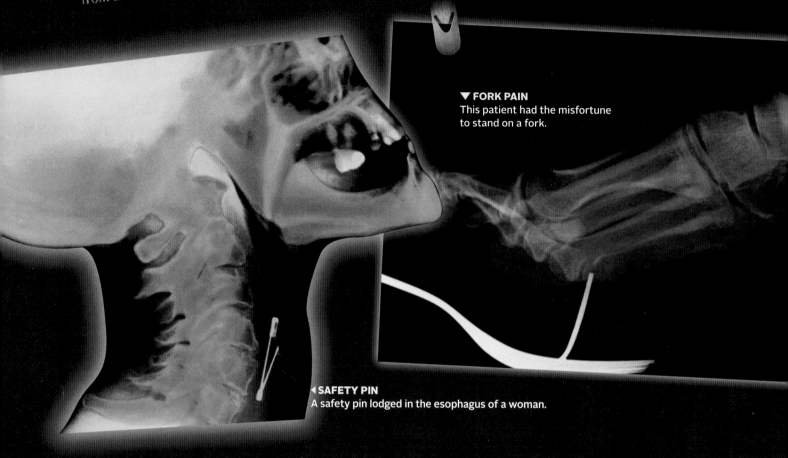

▼ **FORK PAIN**
This patient had the misfortune to stand on a fork.

◄ **SAFETY PIN**
A safety pin lodged in the esophagus of a woman.

einstein scan An X-ray of Albert Einstein's skull fetched more than $35,000 at a 2010 auction in Beverly Hills, California. The genius scientist had the scan in 1945, ten years before his death at age 76.

botox cure A stroke victim who had been paralyzed for more than 20 years was able to walk again after being injected with Botox, a substance usually associated with smoothing wrinkles. Having been told by doctors that he would never regain his mobility, Russell McPhee of Victoria, Australia, was able to stand up and walk a few yards just a month after his first Botox injection.

chance discovery An X-ray of a 35-year-old woman from Para, Brazil, who complained of earache revealed that she had over 20 steel needles in her body. She had inserted the needles into herself as a child.

fatal pick In September 2008, a man from Manchester, England, died from a nosebleed caused by his aggressive nose picking.

horned man Jesse Thornhill of Tulsa, Oklahoma, has two devil horns on his head, created by surgically implanting Teflon lumps under the skin to stretch the scalp. The heavy-metal fan also boasts tattooed eyebrows, lengthened earlobes, and implant earrings on his head.

echo location A blind English boy has learned to "see" again after adopting a technique used by dolphins and bats to detect where objects are. Jamie Aspland from Ashford, Kent, navigates his way around obstacles by means of echolocation, whereby he utters high-pitch clicks and then interprets the sound that rebounds off the surfaces.

tortoise woman For nearly 30 years, Sun Fengqin from Inner Mongolia carried a 55-lb (25-kg) tumor on her back, which resulted in her being nicknamed "Tortoise Woman." The tumor started as a yellow birthmark but grew so large that in the end she struggled to walk upright.

rubber man Vijay Sharma of Rajasthan, India, is so flexible that he can pass his body through a tennis racket, wind his arms around his back so that his hands grip each other at the front of his waist, wrap his legs over his head, and drink from bottles that he has gripped between his toes.

souvenir finger After losing part of his small finger, Matthew Tipler of Bend, Oregon, took the tip, encased it in clear plastic, and made a keychain out of it.

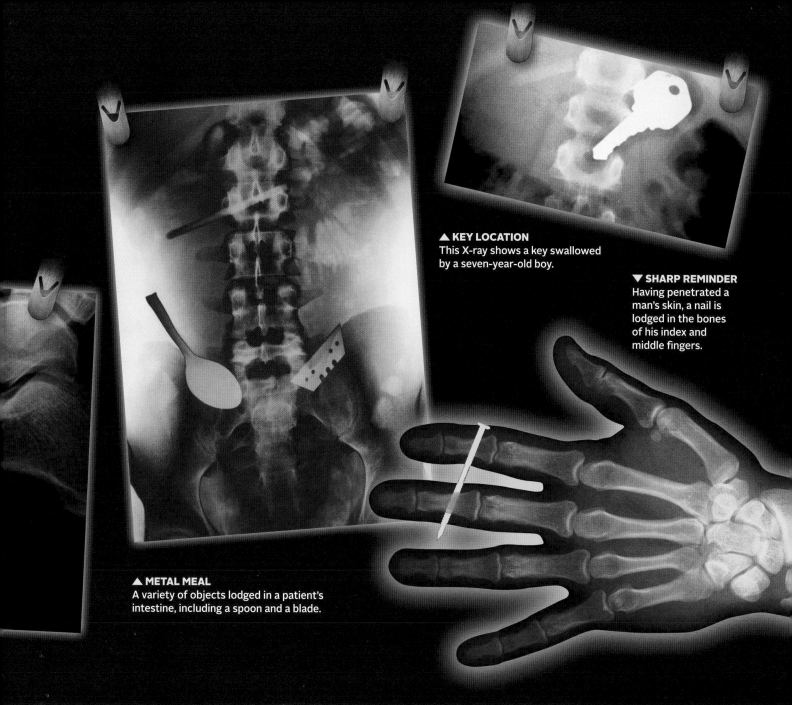

▲ KEY LOCATION
This X-ray shows a key swallowed by a seven-year-old boy.

▼ SHARP REMINDER
Having penetrated a man's skin, a nail is lodged in the bones of his index and middle fingers.

▲ METAL MEAL
A variety of objects lodged in a patient's intestine, including a spoon and a blade.

bumpy landing In June 2009, window cleaner Alex Clay from Eau Claire, Wisconsin, fell six floors, bounced off a concrete first-floor roof, and landed on the ground—surviving with nothing worse than a broken foot bone and a cut on his leg.

amnesia victim In 2009, a man later identified as Edward Lighthart walked out of a park in Seattle, Washington, with $600 in his sock but with no idea of who he was and how he got there—the victim of a rare form of dissociative amnesia.

caught toddler Two-year-old Zhang Fangyu survived a 100-ft (30-m) fall in Hangzhou, Zhejiang Province, China, in June 2011 after she climbed out of a 10th-floor window and was caught by a woman walking in the street below. Her rescuer, Wu Juping, suffered multiple fractures to her arm.

facial transplant Thirty Spanish doctors at the Vall D'Hebron Hospital in Barcelona worked for 22 hours in March 2010 to perform a full facial transplant on a patient, which included skin, nerves, muscles, nose, lips, cheekbones, teeth, and a jawbone. The recipient, a 31-year-old man, is eventually expected to regain up to 90 percent of his facial functions.

foot skills Born without arms, Ren Jiemei from Shandong Province, China, has learned to use her feet to eat, wash, comb her hair, draw pictures, and cut paper. She is so skilled with her feet that when she uses them to thread a needle she is always successful on the first attempt—in fact, she is said to be the best embroiderer in her village. In her school days, she often topped the class despite having to write with her feet and use her mouth to turn book pages.

arm wrestler Joby Mathew from Kerala, India, may be only 3 ft 5 in (1.05 m) tall but he is a champion arm wrestler. Despite having severely underdeveloped legs, he is able to defeat able-bodied opponents who are twice his height. He can also jump up steps using only his hands and perform push-ups on just one hand.

first-aid app During the 65 hours that U.S. filmmaker Dan Woolley was trapped following the Haitian earthquake in January 2010, he used an iPhone first-aid application to treat his fractured leg and head wound.

skydiving champ Despite losing both his legs in a bomb explosion in Northern Ireland in 1992, former paratrooper Alistair Hodgson of Cumbria, England, is a freestyle skydiving champion and has made more than 5,000 jumps.

MINI MAN

At age 22, Wu Kang from Wuhan, China, wears the clothes of a nine-month-old toddler and stands just under 2 ft 3 in (68 cm) tall. Wu suffers from panhypopituitarism, which decreases the secretion of hormones, including growth hormones, produced by the pituitary gland in the brain.

body-building granny At age 73, grandmother Ernestine Shepherd of Baltimore, Maryland, gets up at 3 a.m. and spends her days running, lifting weights, and working out. She runs 80 mi (130 km) a week—the equivalent of three marathons—bench-presses 150 lb (68 kg), and lifts 20-lb (9-kg) dumbbells.

heart stopped Joseph Tiralosi of Brooklyn, New York City, miraculously survived after his heart stopped beating for 45 minutes. The 56-year-old father had gone into sudden cardiac arrest inside the emergency room at New York-Presbyterian/Weill Cornell Medical Center, and it was nearly an hour before doctors succeeded in getting his heart going again. Usually if a person cannot be revived within six minutes, they die. Equally incredible, he came through the whole episode without suffering any form of brain damage.

poke-a-nut During a 2009 martial-arts demonstration in Malacca, Malaysia, Ho Eng Hui pierced four coconuts with his index finger in 31.8 seconds.

mass extraction Between the ages of seven and 12, Chelsea Keysaw of Kinnear, Wyoming, underwent three oral surgeries to remove a total of 13 extra permanent teeth and 15 baby teeth.

turtle boy Maimaiti Hali from Heping, China, was born with a hard, mutated growth covering most of his back, its shell-like appearance leading bullies to call him "Turtle Boy." The growth was removed from the eight-year-old's back in a two-hour operation in 2010 and replaced with skin grafts from his scalp and legs.

second face A baby born in China's Hunan Province has two faces. Kangkang was born in 2009 with a transverse facial cleft that extends nearly all the way up to his ears, making it look as if he is wearing a mask.

free flights Thirty-one-year-old Liew Siaw Hsia gave birth on an AirAsia flight over Malaysia in October 2009, and as a result the company granted her and her child free flights for life.

sandwich bag To keep up the body temperature of a tiny premature baby, medics at Worcestershire Royal Hospital in England used the smallest insulating jacket they could find—a 6-in (15-cm) plastic sandwich bag from the hospital kitchens. The improvised insulator did the trick and saved the life of little Lexi Lacey who had been born 14 weeks early weighing just 14 oz (396 g) and had been given only a ten percent chance of survival.

making antivenom Snake antivenom is commonly produced by injecting horses with snake venom, then collecting the appropriate antibodies from their blood.

rope bed Gao Yang of Liaoning Province, China, can sleep on a single length of rope tied between two trees for up to seven hours at a time. He was taught special balancing skills at age 12 but it took him nearly a quarter of a century to master this feat by practicing on a 10-ft-high (3-m) rope in his local park every morning.

gold tattoo A business in Dubai offers temporary body tattoos made of real gold. The 24-carat gold-leaf tattoos are in demand for glitzy parties and weddings and can be bought for as little as $50. The company is also offering the tattoos in platinum.

BREATHE IN!

Steve McFarlane of South Jordan, Utah, can displace some of his internal organs to suck his stomach in with spectacular effect.

BEFORE

AFTER

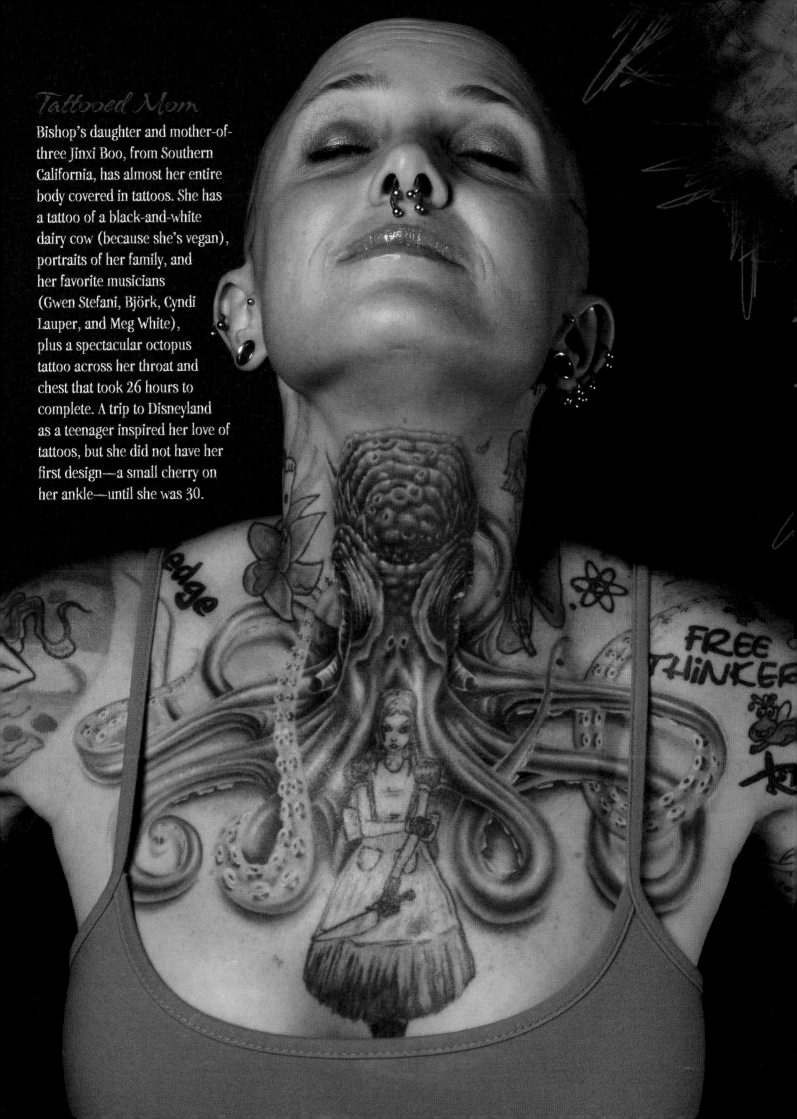

Tattooed Mom

Bishop's daughter and mother-of-three Jinxi Boo, from Southern California, has almost her entire body covered in tattoos. She has a tattoo of a black-and-white dairy cow (because she's vegan), portraits of her family, and her favorite musicians (Gwen Stefani, Björk, Cyndi Lauper, and Meg White), plus a spectacular octopus tattoo across her throat and chest that took 26 hours to complete. A trip to Disneyland as a teenager inspired her love of tattoos, but she did not have her first design—a small cherry on her ankle—until she was 30.

Ripley's Believe It or Not!®

nickel allergy Kim Taylor from Northamptonshire, England, is unable to touch hundreds of everyday items like keys, coins, zippers, scissors, door handles, and saucepans because she is severely allergic to nickel. She takes her own wooden-handled cutlery to restaurants and has to cover everything nickel—even her eyeglasses, bra clasp, and buttons—in nail varnish so that her skin doesn't come into contact with the metal.

extra bones Dan Aziere of Danbury, Connecticut, suffers from multiple hereditary exostoses, a rare genetic disorder that causes extra bones to keep growing in his body. He estimates that he has about 50 excess bones—some as large as 4 in (10 cm) long—and since the age of five he has had more than a dozen operations to remove them.

name jinx The parents of a boy who has failed to grow since being born on Dwarf Street claim the name has jinxed their child. Four-year-old Liu Chengrui from Wuhan, China, still weighs just 11 lb (5 kg) and stands only 2 ft (60 cm) tall.

eye twitch Barbara Watkins of Halifax, England, suffers from a rare and bizarre condition that causes her to wink thousands of times a day. She has blepharospasm, an incurable condition that causes frequent muscle contractions around the eyes and affects just a handful of people in every million.

BEARDED LADY

When she suddenly started to grow facial hair in the 1920s, Mrs. Baker B. Twyman of Peoria, Illinois, supported her family by joining the circus as a bearded lady. She later had the surplus hair surgically removed.

miracle boy Seventeen-month-old Jessiah Jackson of Leland, North Carolina, fell from a chair in July 2010 and a metal hook pierced his skull. It penetrated 2 in (5 cm) into his brain, but he survived.

high life Husband and wife Wayne and Laurie Hallquist of Stockton, California, measure a combined height of 13 ft 4 in (4.07 m). He stands 6 ft 10 in (2.1 m) and she is 6 ft 6 in (1.97 m).

hidden needle Doctors in China's Henan Province removed a needle from a man's brain that may have been there for 50 years. Following a seizure, Lin Yaohui, 51, was rushed to hospital where X-rays revealed the 2-in-long (5-cm) metal needle embedded in his skull. As an adult's skull is hard, surgeons believe the needle must have penetrated his head before he was 18 months old.

sneezed bullet A man who was shot in the head during New Year's Eve celebrations in Naples, Italy, survived after sneezing the bullet out of his nose. The .22 calibre bullet went through the right side of Darco Sangermano's head, behind his eye socket, and lodged in his nasal passage. Bleeding heavily, he was rushed to a hospital but while waiting to be seen by doctors, he sneezed and the bullet flew out of his right nostril.

tiny tot At 21 years old, Hatice Kocaman from Kadirli, Turkey, has the body mass of an eight-month-old baby. She suffers from a rare bone disease and stands just 28 in (70 cm) tall and weighs only 15 lb (6.8 kg).

TALL TEEN

At age 14, Brazilian teenager Elisany Silva towers over her sisters because she is already 6 ft 9 in (2.06 m) tall. She is so tall that she had to stop going to school because she could not fit on the bus. Medical experts believe she could be suffering from gigantism, a condition in which the body produces excessive amounts of growth hormones. If left untreated she could continue to grow up to 6 in (15 cm) more a year.

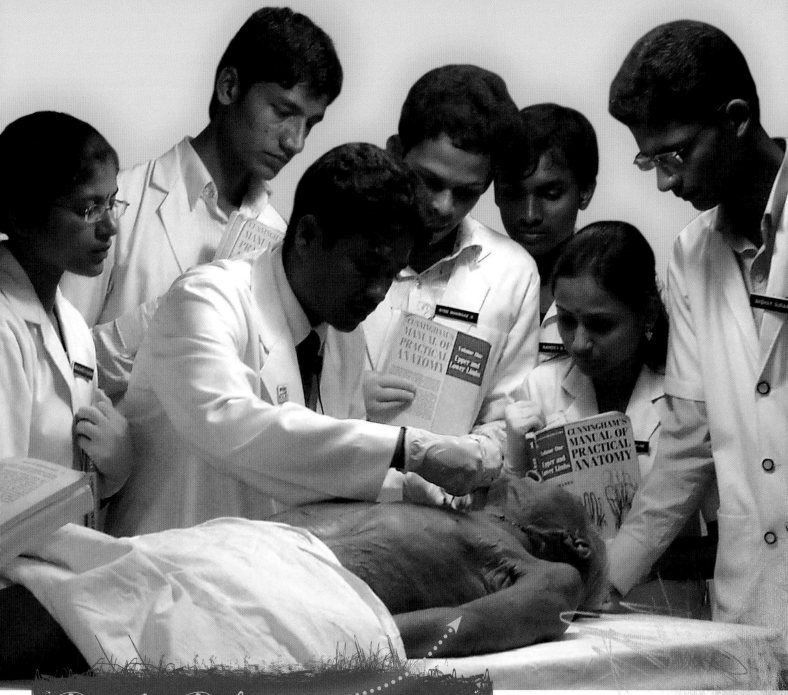

Dissecting Dad

To help teach anatomy to his students, Dr. Mahantesh Ramannavar dissected the body of his father, Dr. Basavanneppa Ramannavar, which had been embalmed for exactly two years. His father had specified in his will that his body should be donated to the university in Belgaum, India, where his son worked and that his son should perform the dissection, which was shown live on Indian TV.

turning the screw After an operation to remove a tumor left a gaping hole in his leg, 14-year-old Simeon Fairburn from Brisbane, Australia, saved the limb by turning surgical screws on a leg brace four times every day for over two years to stretch the bone by 1 ft (30 cm). He initially faced amputation, but after wearing the brace and undergoing 20 operations, he still has a chance of achieving his dream and becoming a basketball player.

skewered neck Twelve-year-old Garret Mullikin from Houston, Texas, survived after a 9-in-long (23-cm) stick skewered his neck. Falling off a dirt bike, he hit the ground and the piece of tree branch, as thick as a broom handle, plunged into his neck and down into his chest, through his lung, past vital arteries and his heart. Doctors said that if the stick had been pulled out before he was rushed to hospital, he could have bled to death.

serial sleeper Claire Allen from Cambridge, England, falls asleep 100 times a day. Her condition—an extreme form of narcolepsy—causes her to fall into a trancelike state where she is unable to see or move. Each episode lasts between 30 seconds and five minutes and is triggered by emotions such as surprise and anger, and especially surfaces when she laughs.

worm's-eye view After John Matthews of Bellevue, Iowa, noticed two spots obscuring the vision in his left eye, doctors diagnosed the cause—a worm had got into his eye. The worm—thought to be either a hookworm or a raccoon roundworm—was then killed by medics who shot a laser into his left eyeball. "I could see it from behind," he said, "moving, trying to dodge the laser."

Ripley's Believe It or Not!® body tales

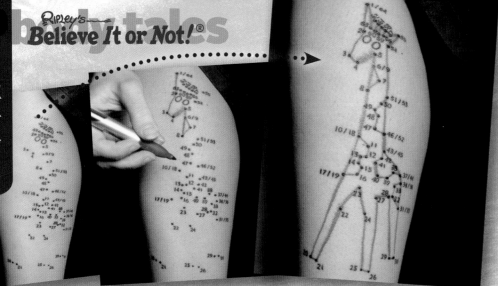

JOIN THE DOTS

Inspired by the idea of getting her birthmarks numbered, Colleen A.F. Venable from New York City has a connect-the-dots tattoo that creates the shape of a giraffe on her left leg.

nose leech *Tyrannobdella rex*, a new species of leech with savage, sawlike teeth, was first discovered in the nose of a nine-year-old Peruvian girl. Named after the most ferocious dinosaur in history, the 2-in (5-cm) bloodsucker came to light after the girl, who regularly swam in tropical rivers and lakes, complained of feeling a sliding sensation in one of her nostrils.

free leg Needing a $60,000 bionic leg so that he could walk again, David Huckvale of Leicestershire, England, happened to go to his local pub on the same day as surgeon Alistair Gibson, who specializes in fitting the computer-controlled limbs. When the two got talking, Mr. Gibson mentioned he had a spare leg and could fit it for free!

hiccup cure After hiccupping an estimated 20 million times over a period of three years, Chris Sands of Lincolnshire, England, finally stopped in 2009 following brain surgery. It is thought that a tumor on his brain stem had been pushing on nerves, causing him to hiccup every two seconds, 24 hours a day.

diamond tattoo South African jeweler Yair Shimansky designed a temporary tattoo made of 612 diamonds and carrying a price tag of $924,000. It took more than eight hours to encrust the ornate floral design on the skin of a model using a special water-based adhesive.

rare phenomenon A woman who had been pronounced dead hours earlier at a hospital in Cali, Colombia, following a series of unsuccessful resuscitation attempts, suddenly started breathing again in a funeral home as workers began to apply formaldehyde to her body. Doctors later diagnosed her condition as a case of Lazarus Syndrome, an extremely rare phenomenon in which the body's circulation spontaneously restarts after failed resuscitations.

changing beard Sameer Mehta, a businessman from Gujarat, India, makes weekly trips to the barber and has had more than 60 styles of short beard in the last four years. These have included a heart-shaped beard and another trimmed in the design of his country's flag.

rod removed While playing on a construction site, 12-year-old Kalim Ali from Malegaon, India, was skewered by a rod 3 ft 4 in (1 m) long that pierced ten internal organs, including his rectum, small intestine, lungs, and liver. Incredibly, the 0.6-in-thick (1.5-cm) pole didn't damage any major blood vessels, and surgeons successfully removed it after a three-hour operation.

26 digits Heramb Ashok Kumthekar from Goa, India, has six fingers on each hand and seven toes on each foot, giving him a total of 26 digits. He is proud of his condition, called polydactylism, even though he has insufficient nerve endings to feel all his fingers and toes.

tall teen At just 16 years old, schoolgirl Marvadene Anderson stood 6 ft 11 in (2.1 m) tall, making the New Jersey school basketball star 5 in (12.5 cm) taller than her idol, Michael Jordan. Height must run in the family because the Jamaican-born teenager's older sister, Kimberly, is 6 ft 4 in (1.9 m) tall.

bullet in head After being shot at point-blank range by a German soldier in 1944, Ivan Nikulin of Chita, Russia, lived happily with a bullet lodged in his head for nearly 70 years.

latin tattoos As a subject, Latin is ten times more popular in British schools than it was a decade ago. One theory for the ancient language's surge in popularity is that it is because celebrities such as Angelina Jolie, David Beckham, and Colin Farrell have body tattoos with Latin inscriptions.

body piercing In April 2010, Ed Bruns of Gillette, Wyoming, had more than 1,500 16-gauge needles inserted into his arms, back, and legs by a body-piercing artist in less than 4½ hours.

tattoo proposal When San Diego, California, tattoo artist Joe Wittenberg decided to propose to his girlfriend, he inked the words "Rachel, will you marry me?" on his own leg.

organs awry Bethany Jordan from the West Midlands, England, was born with her internal organs in unexpected places in her body. Her heart is behind her lungs, her liver and stomach are on the opposite side of her body from normal, and she has five tiny spleens instead of just one.

Furry Features

Supatra Sasuphan from Bangkok, Thailand,
was born with Ambras Syndrome—or
congenital hypertrichosis—a rare genetic
disease that causes excessive hair growth on
the face and other parts of the body. It affects
one person in a billion, and there are fewer
than 40 known cases in the world. There is
no permanent cure for the condition, but
nine-year-old Supatra doesn't let it affect her
life and enjoys the same activities as
her schoolfriends. She hopes eventually
to become a teacher.

ACKNOWLEDGMENTS

COVER (t/l) Nick Afanasiev, (r) Asha Mandela; 4 Joey Miller; 7 (t/c) NY Daily News via Getty Images, (t/r) Getty Images; 8 (t) Charles Eisenmann Collection/University of Syracuse, (b) Xinhua/Photoshot; 9 Christine Cornege/AP/Press Association Images; 10 (t) Chuck Nyce, (b) Quirky China News/Rex Features; 11 Reuters/China Daily China Daily Information Corp – CDIC; 12–13 Alan Humerose/Rezo.ch; 14 (t) Collection of Jack and Beverly Wilgus, (b) © Europics; 15 Asha Mandela; 16 (t) Chad Grochowski, (b) Bob Huberman; 17 (t) Dennis Van Tine/ABACA USA/Empics Entertainment, (b) Anders (The Piercing Guy) Allinger www.phatpiercings.com; 18 Sinopix/Rex Features; 19 (b/l, c) Nick Afanasiev, (t/r) Basit Umer/Barcroft Media Ltd; 20 Steve Gschmeissner/Science Photo Library; 21 Image courtesy of the New England Journal of Medicine; 22 Circus World Museum, Baraboo, Wisconsin; 24 (t) Quirky China News/Rex Features, (c/l, b/l) Tejnaksh Healthcare's Institute of Urology, (b/r) EPA/Photoshot; 25 Atlas Press/eyevine; 26 (l) Science Photo Library, (r) Du Cane Medical Imaging Ltd/Science Photo Library; 27 (l) Science Photo Library, (t/r) Scott Camazine/Science Photo Library, (b/r) Kaj R. Svensson/Science Photo Library; 28 (t) © Europics [CEN], (b) Pictures courtesy of Steve McFarlane; 29 Mario Rosenau/Bizarre archive/Dennis Publishing; 30 (t) Getty Images, (b) Reuters/Paulo Santos; 31 KPN; 32 (t) Joey Millerr

Key: t = top, b = bottom, c = center, l = left, r = right, sp = single page, dp = double page

All other photos are from Ripley Entertainment Inc.
Every attempt has been made to acknowledge correctly and contact copyright holders and we apologize in advance
for any unintentional errors or omissions, which will be corrected in future editions.